Healthy Plates

BEING FIT

VALERIE BODDEN

Published by Creative Education and Creative Paperbacks | P.O. Box 227, Mankato, Minnesota 56002
Creative Education and Creative Paperbacks are imprints of The Creative Company
www.thecreativecompany.us

Design and production by Liddy Walseth | Printed in the United States of America

Photographs by Corbis (Kevin Dodge, Imaginechina, Kam & Co./cultura, Beau Lark), Dreamstime
(David Kelly, Yen Hung Lin, Szefei), Getty Images (Kemter, kristian sekulic, Merten Snijders,
VisualCommunications), iStockphoto (AlbertSmirnov, MaszaS, olgysha2008, skynesher),
Shutterstock (Andrey_Kuzmin, Nanette Grebe, Pavel Hlystov, KimPinPhotography, KIM NGUYEN)

Library of Congress Cataloging-in-Publication Data
Bodden, Valerie. | Being fit / Valerie Bodden. | p. cm. — (Healthy plates) | Summary: An early reader's
introduction to the connections between being fit and staying healthy, benefits of aerobic exercises
such as biking, nutritional concepts such as calories, and recipe instructions. | Includes bibliographi-
cal references and index. | ISBN 978-1-60818-506-1 (hardcover) | ISBN 978-1-62832-106-7 (pbk)
1. Physical fitness—Juvenile literature. I. Title. | RA781.B58 2015 | 613.7—dc23 | 2014000705

CCSS: RI.1.1, 2, 4, 5, 6, 7; RI.2.2, 5, 6, 7, 10; RI.3.1, 5, 7, 8; RF.1.1, 3, 4; RF.2.3, 4

First Edition 9 8 7 6 5 4 3 2 1

TABLE OF CONTENTS

Fit and Active

Being fit means being healthy. When you are fit, your body works well. You have the energy you need to be active. Your body is at a healthy weight.

WATER SPORTS SUCH AS SURFING CAN BE A FUN WAY TO STAY FIT.

Five Food Groups

Kids who are fit eat healthy foods from the five food groups. They eat fruits and vegetables, dairy foods, **grains**, and **proteins** like meat or nuts. Fit kids exercise almost every day.

FRUITS AND VEGETABLES ARE THE MOST COLORFUL FOODS ON YOUR PLATE.

Exercise for Fitness

It's easy to exercise! All you have to do is play. You can play soccer or go swimming. You can ride your bike, jump rope, or dance to your favorite music. Running and walking are great exercises, too!

SWIMMING IS A TYPE OF EXERCISE YOU CAN ENJOY BY YOURSELF OR WITH FRIENDS.

Exercises like running or biking are called aerobic (*eh-RO-bik*) exercises. Aerobic exercises make your heart and lungs strong. They also help your body burn **calories** from food. This helps you keep a healthy body weight.

You can do exercises to make your muscles stronger, too. Crunches or sit-ups build up your stomach muscles. Pushups strengthen your arm muscles. So does swinging across the monkey bars!

CLIMBING THE JUNGLE GYM AT THE PARK CAN BE EXERCISE!

Stretching exercises are important, too. They help make your body **flexible** so that you will not get hurt easily. Bending over to touch your toes is a good stretch.

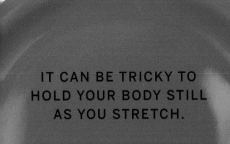

IT CAN BE TRICKY TO HOLD YOUR BODY STILL AS YOU STRETCH.

Why Be Fit?

Learning how to be fit now can help you stay healthy later. Exercise can make it easier for you to pay attention at school, too. It can help you have more energy and sleep better. Exercising can even make you feel happier.

Tips for Success

Warm up your body slowly when you are exercising. Then you can work harder. Make sure to drink plenty of water while you exercise.

SWINGING CAN BE A GOOD WAY TO WARM UP—OR COOL DOWN.

Most kids need about an hour of exercise every day. But you do not have to get all your exercise at once. You can run around the playground at recess and ride your bike after school. You can even do pushups as you watch TV. Anytime you can get your body moving, you will be making yourself fit!

YOU CAN EXERCISE OUTDOORS OR INSIDE, WITH FRIENDS OR BY YOURSELF.

MAKE A FIT SNACK:

TRAIL MIX

1 HANDFUL RAISINS
1 HANDFUL PEANUTS OR
SUNFLOWER SEEDS
1 HANDFUL CHEERIOS
1 HANDFUL CHOCOLATE CHIPS

Put all the ingredients in a zip-top bag. Shake to mix. Eat your trail mix, and you will have plenty of energy to exercise!

GLOSSARY

calories—a way of measuring the energy in food; eating too many calories and not exercising can make a person gain weight

flexible—able to bend easily

grains—parts of some kinds of grasses, such as wheat or oats, that are used to make bread and other foods

proteins—foods such as meat and nuts that contain the nutrient protein, which helps the body grow

READ MORE

Head, Honor. *Keeping Fit.* Mankato, Minn.: Sea-to-Sea, 2013.

Read, Leon. *Make It Move.* Mankato, Minn.: Sea-to-Sea, 2011.

Royston, Angela. *Why Do I Run?* Mankato, Minn.: QEB, 2010.

WEBSITES

CDC: BAM! Body and Mind

http://www.cdc.gov/bam/activity/index.html

Find new ideas for ways to get moving and be fit.

Kids.gov: Exercise and Eating Healthy

http://kids.usa.gov/exercise-and-eating-healthy/index.shtml

Learn more about healthy foods and exercise, and play a game about being fit.

Note: Every effort has been made to ensure that the websites listed above are suitable for children, that they have educational value, and that they contain no inappropriate material. However, because of the nature of the Internet, it is impossible to guarantee that these sites will remain active indefinitely or that their contents will not be altered.

INDEX